A New True Book

DINOSAURS

By Mary Lou Clark

This "true book" was prepared under the direction of Illa Podendorf, formerly with the Laboratory School, University of Chicago

Plesiosaurus

PHOTO CREDITS
Richard Wahl—4,6,7,8,9,10,13,14,17,18,19,20,22,23,26,30,31,32,34,36,37
Field Museum of Natural History, Chicago—2,28
James P. Rowan—cover, 24 (2 photos), 44 (top)
Reinhard Brucker—39
National Museum of Natural History, Smithsonian Institution—40 (top), 44 (bottom)
Connecticut Department of Economic Development—40 (bottom)
U.S. Department of Interior, National Park Service: Dinosaur National Monument—43
Cover—Life-size model of Triceratops at the Smithsonian Institution, Washington D.C.

Library of Congress Cataloging in Publication Data
Clark, Mary Lou.
Dinosaurs.
(A New True book)
Previously published as: The true book of dinosaurs. 1955.
SUMMARY: Briefly describes a number of different dinosaurs, what came before and after them, why they disappeared, and how we have learned about them.
1. Dinosaurs—Juvenile literature. [1. Dinosaurs] I. Title.
QE862.D5C54 1981 567.9'1 81-7750
ISBN 0-516-01612-1 AACR2

14 15 16 17 18 19 R 93

TABLE OF CONTENTS

APATOSAURUS
TYRANNOSAURUS REX
TRICERATOPS
STEGOSAURUS
CORYTHOSAURUS
DIPLODOCUS
MODERN HORSE

DINOSAURS

The word dinosaur means "Terrible Lizard."

Years and years ago, more than you can count, these great animals lived on the earth.

There were no people then.

APATOSAURUS

"Deceptive Lizard" was as big as ten elephants. It was a plant eater.

Deceptive Lizard has another name—Apatosaurus. Apatosaurus means "Deceptive Lizard." It was once called Brontosaurus—or "Thunder Lizard."

Some of the time, Deceptive Lizards stood in the water. They ate the plants that grew there. Four big legs helped the Deceptive Lizards hold up their heavy bodies.

"Longest Lizard" looked a great deal like Deceptive Lizard. It was a plant eater, too.

Can you imagine how big it was?

DIPLODOCUS

Measure a string eighty times as long as this picture. This is how big Longest Lizard was.

STEGOSAURUS

"Armored Lizard" lived on land. It was a plant eater.

Armored Lizard had hard plates of bone along its back. These plates of bone helped protect it from meat eaters.

There was a “Leaping Lizard.” It lived on land. It was a meat eater.

ALLOSAURUS

ALLOSAURUS
FIGHTING
APATOSAURUS

The meat eaters were enemies of the plant eaters.

The meat eaters went after the Deceptive Lizards when they came out of the water.

Deceptive Lizards were too heavy to run away. They had only their tails and teeth to fight with.

Often they lost to the meat eaters.

Millions and millions of years went by. Slowly changes took place.

The first of the dinosaurs disappeared from the earth. But other dinosaurs appeared.

"Tyrant King" was the most fierce of all. Tyrant King was a meat eater. He had big jaws and sharp teeth.

TYRANNOSAURUS REX

"Duck-billed Lizard" had a mouth shaped like a duck's. It had many rows of teeth.

One of the smaller plant-eating dinosaurs had a sharp beak.

It had a shield-shaped skull bone at the back of its head, too.

Its beak, teeth, and skull helped protect it from the meat-eating dinosaurs.

TRICERATOPS

"Three-horned Face" had three horns. It had a shield-shaped bone in back of its head. Horn-faced lizards were plant eaters. They used their horns to fight off the fierce Tyrant King.

PLESIOSAURUS

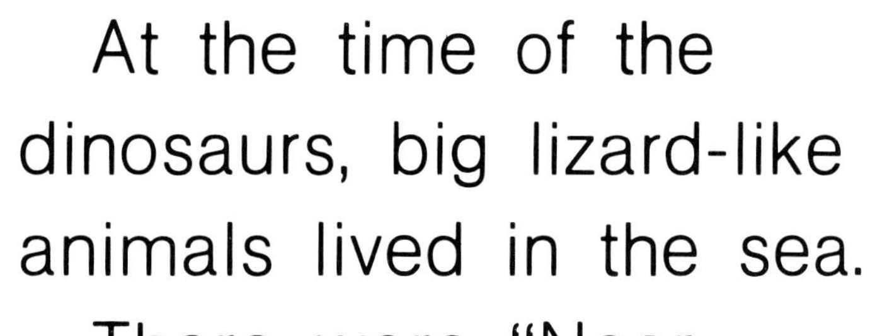

At the time of the dinosaurs, big lizard-like animals lived in the sea.

There were "Near Lizards" with long necks.

There were "Fish Lizards" that were more like fish.

ICHTHYOSAUR

American Alligator

Iguana

Millions and millions of years went by. The earth changed. The weather changed. The big dinosaurs did not change fast enough. They died.

Now there are no dinosaurs. But there are animals living today that belong to the same group of animals as the dinosaurs. Some reptiles are like dinosaurs.

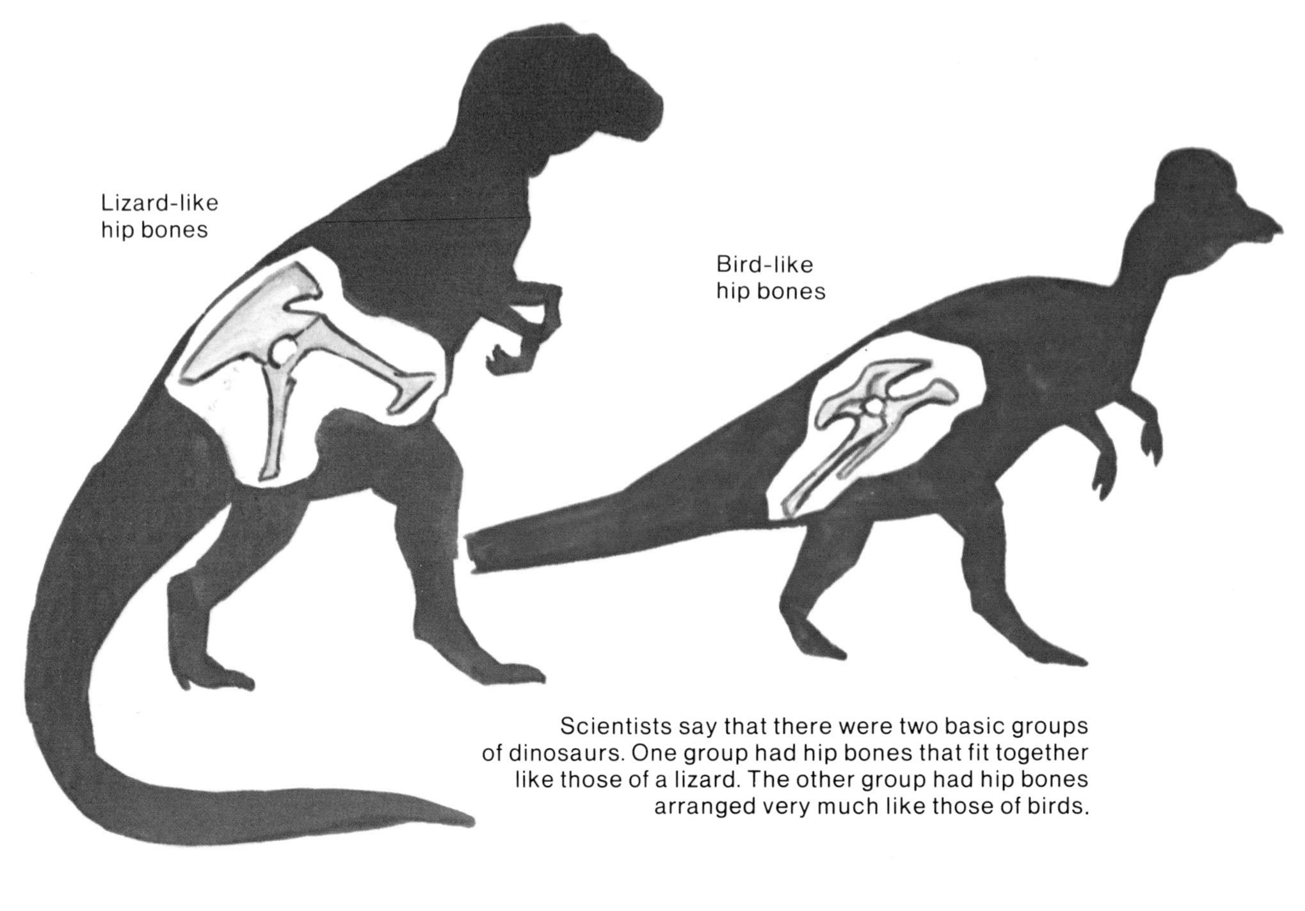

Scientists say that there were two basic groups of dinosaurs. One group had hip bones that fit together like those of a lizard. The other group had hip bones arranged very much like those of birds.

Many birds are like other dinosaurs, especially the small meat eaters.

Today many scientists think dinosaurs were closest to the bird family.

WHAT CAME BEFORE THE DINOSAURS?

Before there were dinosaurs, there were many other kinds of animals. Some lived in the sea. Some lived on land.

The very first animals lived in the sea. They were small. Many of them had shells.

Later there were fish.
One of the biggest of these was the "Terrible Fish."

"Drawn-out Face" was one of the first animals to walk on land. It had smooth skin. It could live in water and on land.

DIMETRODON

Many years before the dinosaurs appeared there was a "Sail-Back" animal that lived on land.

EARLY
MAMMALS

The dinosaurs laid eggs. They often left the eggs to hatch, just as some reptiles do today.

Before the dinosaurs disappeared, there were some small animals called mammals. Mammals are animals that give birth to their young. They feed their young milk. Sometimes mammals have to fight to keep their young safe.

MAMMOTH
MASTODON

SABER-TOOTHED TIGER

WHAT CAME AFTER THE DINOSAURS?

After all the dinosaurs were gone there were large mammals on the earth. Now, some of these are gone, too.

FOSSILS: STORIES IN STONE

If there were no people in the world, how do we know about these animals of long ago?

Many animals have left a story. The story is found in the layers of rock of the earth.

Digging for dinosaur bones in Utah.

This North American mastodon lived from coast to coast from Alaska to Mexico.

Dinosaur footprints in Connecticut

Animals died and left their bones. They left their footprints. Many of these bones and footprints have been found. They had been changed to stone. They are called fossils.

People study the fossils. A rock with a fossil in it may be sent to a museum. In the museum the fossils are set up so that many people can see them.

Fossils tell us about the size of the dinosaurs. They tell us what dinosaurs probably ate.

Scientist digs out dinosaur bones in Dinosaur National Monument.

Camarasaurus

Fossil of a saber-toothed tiger found in California

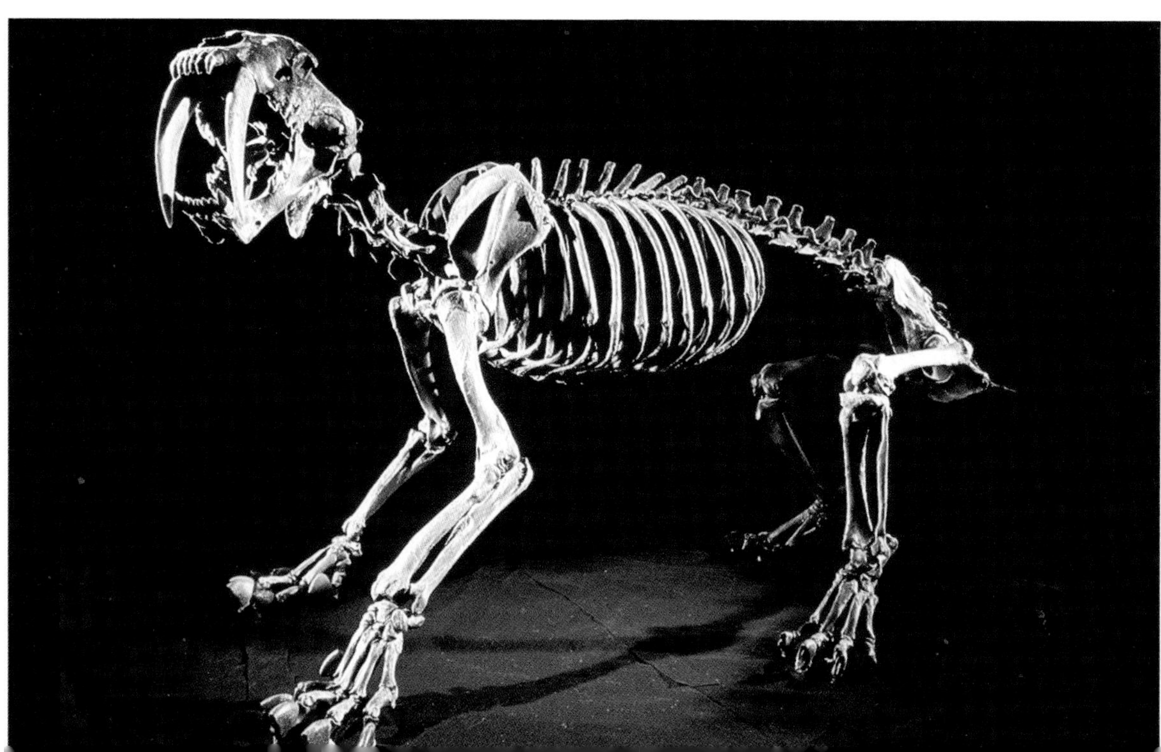

There is still much of the story to be found out. Dinosaurs are only a small part of a much bigger story, the story of our earth and how it changed.

Someday you will want to read more of the story that fossils tell.

WORDS YOU SHOULD KNOW

appear(uh • PEER)—to be seen
armoured(ARE • merrd)—covered with a heavy covering like shells or plates
beak(BEEK)—bill; the hard parts of a mouth
deceptive(dih • SEP • tihv)—misleading; not what it seems to be
dinosaur(DY • nuh • sore)—a kind of animal that lived long ago
disappear(dis • uh • PEER)—not be seen; vanish
duck-billed(DUK • billd)—shaped with a broad, flat bill like a duck's
earth(ERTH)—our world; the planet on which we live
enemy(EN • uh • mee)—not a friend
especially(es • PESH • uh • lee)—in a special way; more than usually
fierce(FEERSS)—dangerous; wild; mean
fossil(FOSS • ill)—the remains of plants and animals that lived long ago
great(GRAYT)—big; very large
heavy(HEV • ee)—having much weight
horn—hard, pointed growth on some animals' heads
jaw—the upper and lower parts of the mouth
layer—a thickness
leaping(LEE • ping)—jumping
lizard(LIZ • erd)—an animal with four legs, a tail, and a body covered with scales; a reptile
mammal(MAM • ihl)—an animal covered with hair or fur
measure(MEH • zher)—to figure the size of something
museum(myu • ZEE • um)—a building for keeping and showing interesting and valuable things

plate—a hard, bony covering of an animal
probably (PROB • ub • lee)—likely to happen
protect (proh • TEKT)—to keep safe; guard
reptile (REP • tyl)—a cold-blooded animal with a backbone and covered with scales or plates
row—placed in a line
sail-backed (SAYL • bakd)—shaped like a sail
sea (SEE)—a body of salt water
sharp—pointed
shell—hard outer covering of some animals
shield-shaped (SHEELD-shaypd)—in the shape of a shield—usually three-sided
smooth—not rough; even
terrible (TAIR • ih • buhl)—not pleasant; fearful; bad
thunder (THUN • der)—loud noise
tyrant (TY • rent)—cruel; not nice

INDEX

About the Author

Mary Lou Clark earned her Master of Science degree at the University of Pittsburgh and her Ph.D. degree at San Diego State University. She has taught high school chemistry and physics and once hosted a TV science show for children. Married and the mother of four children, Mrs. Clark has written numerous magazine articles and stories both for juvenile and adult readers.